My Freshman Manual

My Freshman Manual

(The Official College Handbook)

by

Joseph P. Turton

My Freshman Manual
by Joseph P. Turton
Copyright © 1995 by Joseph P. Turton

Library of Congress # 94-090716

ISBN # 0-9644302-0-7

Cover Art by Tobin Troyer: Freelance Illustrator

Published by:

Creative Publishing
Joseph P. Turton
27409 Detroit Rd., Apt. G-3
Westlake, Ohio 44145

*This book is dedicated to
my Mom, Dad, and
little brother
Bobby.*

Introduction

Is it fat or is it thin? Which college is it from? Open it! No! Let me! Don't let anyone touch it! These will be some of the most commonly asked questions and emotions you will experience when you receive an acceptance or rejection letter from one of the many colleges that you may have applied to. Finally you open it. Yes! I got accepted! "All right!" you say to yourself. "No more worries. I'm on my way!"

Five months later, when you are getting ready for college, all of those worries that you thought you left behind have suddenly turned into new ones. Will I fit in? What should I or shouldn't I bring? I don't want to stand out too much! What's my roommate going to be like? Will we get along? **CAN I SURVIVE COLLEGE LIFE?**

All of these are common concerns among incoming college freshman. No matter how calm, cool, or collected they act, these questions and concerns are always in the back of their minds, just as they are on your mind right now.

I have written this book in an effort to alleviate many of the potential problems that incoming college freshman may experience as they approach the academic school year. This book focuses on some of the questions and concerns that any new college student might have. It covers information ranging from various social and academic aspects of college life to certain "Rules of Thumb" that are needed for college survival.

In my four years of college life, I had many difficult experiences that I was forced to struggle through. As I was confronted with these challenges, I would write down short helpful hints that would help me solve some of those problems. I would often share these with my fellow students, and they were always appreciated. This became the basis for *My*

Freshman Manual. This book is a simple and basic collection of those helpful hints. It will save time and assist new college freshman in many ways. It helped me and my friends, and I hope it can do the same for you!

Congratulations
and
Good Luck!

1

Bring quarters—Laundry is bad enough, but it's even worse when you don't have enough quarters to get the job done.

2

Get a phone card for calling home. It will save you a lot of money, and you won't have an excuse for not calling Mom and Dad.

3

Know your neighbors—There is always something you don't have, and it's easier to borrow from a friend.

4
Balance your time—It will enable you to do more.

5
Don't expect to be best friends with your roommate. It's o.k. just to get along.

6
Get a word processor or computer rather than an electric typewriter—There is no telling how many times you will have to rewrite a paper.

7
Always keep stamps in your room—It's not always easy to find one when you need it.

8
Have a deck of cards—Every night isn't a party.

9
Bring aspirin!

10
Have a family picture, and keep it on your desk—You will always appreciate it when you are feeling homesick or lonely.

11

Have an address book—Keep in touch with old friends and relatives. You'll always see them again.

12
Watch what you eat—Don't gain the "Freshman Fifteen"!

13
RECYCLE—Be responsible to the environment!

14

Get a calendar or some type of date book—It's too difficult to remember all of the important dates and the various activities that you will be involved in.

15
Buy an alarm clock that has a battery back up—The power always seems to go out in the middle of the night.

16
Set your clock 5 to 10 minutes fast—It will help you get to class on time.

17

Buy a refrigerator rather than renting one—You'll save yourself some money in the long run, and you can always sell it to a new incoming Freshman.

18

Bring an extra lamp or some type of desk light—the dorm rooms are never bright enough.

19

Buy all of your pens, pencils, and notebooks at home—It's cheaper and you don't really need your school logo on everything you own.

20

Bring mouthwash—It works fairly well when you run out of toothpaste, and you never know when you might have an unexpected guest.

21
Bring a camera with you—College is one of the best times in your life and it is nice to have something to look back at after you've graduated.

22
Have a baseball cap—Sundays are usually not big shower days (Especially after a long Saturday night).

23
Create some type of filing system for your papers—It will help you stay organized.

24

Join an organization—A fraternity, sorority, or student government, etc. It will give you a sense of belonging.

25

Get to know the professors in your major department—Letters of recommendation are very useful when you are looking for a job.

26
When you fill out your maintenance room report at the beginning of the year, mark *every single detail* as well as a few extra—School fines can be outrageous for very small damages to your room.

27
Bring an answering machine—It's nice to get phone calls, and the ones that you do get, you'll want to hear.

28
Join an intramural sports team—It's good exercise and you'll meet new people.

29
Save all of your old tests and exams no matter how bad you may have done—
They will be very useful to you later on, as well as to other people when studying for exams.

30
Have extra bath towels—You'll never know what you will have to wipe up.

31
Use common sense—College is no different than anything else in life.

32
Don't expect mail everyday.

33
Know someone who is 21!

34
Write letters so you get mail!

35
Have at least one dressy outfit—There's always an unexpected social event and it's nice to be prepared.

36
Bring your favorite pillow—Unless you like sleeping on plastic pillows.

37
Get to know someone with a car—It will make things easier.

38
Register for your classes as soon as possible—Nothing is worse than getting closed out of a class that you need for your major.

39
Bring notecards for studying—They make good quick reference items.

40
Bring empty milk crates—They are great for storage as well as to use as a file box.

41

Always look your professors directly in the eyes when they are lecturing—It lets them know that you're paying attention.

42
Develop your own set of study habits—
Learn how **you** study best!

43
Don't get cable or the movie channel—
You won't get much homework done.

44
Buy a book on how to make drinks—
You'll be the most popular person
at parties.

45
Try to test out of as many general
requirement classes as possible—
Otherwise, they just get in the way.

46
Bring as many extension cords as you can—Nothing ever reaches quite as far as you think it will.

47
Bring a trunk or storage box—A lot of junk accumulates in college.

48

Buy a student directory—You will be working in a lot of study groups and it is nice when you can get in touch with fellow students.

49

Schedule your classes earlier on during the day so your afternoons are free.

50
Call home every Sunday—Your family misses you too!

51
Have plastic silverware—It's better than using your fingers.

52
Have a credit card—For emergency use only!

53
Have a checking account as well as a savings account—Only use one!

54
Know your own limits—Anything can be done, as long as it's done in moderation.

55
Don't drink too much!

56
Bring a pair of old shoes.

57
While in Washington,
take advantage of what the
city has to offer—Go visit
the monuments.

58
If possible, live on campus all four years (or five or six) of school—You'll have plenty of time to live off campus after you graduate.

59

Mark all of your tapes and cds with
your initials or some type of symbol—
Things always get switched around and
it avoids confusion.

60

If you are going to put up pictures and posters, don't use tacks or nails. You'll get fined for it—Use rubber sticky tack.

61

Budget the money that you made in the summer for each semester—You will spend it faster than you made it!

62
Have a good dictionary.

63
Avoid leaving cheesy messages on your
answering machine.

64
Talk to upperclassmen and ask about a professor before taking a class—A bad professor can ruin a class no matter how interested you are in the material.

65
Get a faculty advisor in your major and be their friend, not just their student.

66
Bring a coffee maker or tea bags—
Caffeine gets you through the nights.

67
Have extra greeting cards around to
send to friends and relatives for
special occasions.

68
Have the number of the local pizza delivery restaurant close to the phone for your late night munchies.

69
It's nice to have some type of small plastic basket to carry all of your toiletries into the showers with.

70
If you are thinking about getting a couch
or chair for your room, get a futon—It
will be your best investment because you
never know who will need to stay over.

71
Don't forget razors and shaving cream.

72
White out!

73
Bring another phone or phone cord—
3 to 4 feet just doesn't allow you
enough room to pace.

74
Have some type of small tool kit—
Things are always breaking and school
maintenance takes forever.

75
Look at the dates of exams—Especially
before scheduling plane tickets.

76
If you haven't worn it in a year, don't
bring it!

77
Buy used books—Not only are they
cheaper, but the important facts and
information just kind of jump out at you.

78
Sit in the front rows of your classes—It will help you pay more attention.

79
Make someone look over your work before you turn it in—You'll tend to overlook the ovious.

80
Have a large duffel bag for small trips.

81
Bring a fan—You may live on the top floor and there isn't always air conditioning.

82
Do an internship in the field that you
wish to work in—It will help prevent you
from making a bad decision.

83
Bring a flashlight.

84
Bring a pencil sharpener—No one else
will have one.

85
Treat your first semester like it's your last and your last semester like it's your first.

86
Put together some type of first aid kit.

87
Bring rubberbands and paper clips—You
never seem to have them when you
need them.

88
Have your parents schedule hotel
reservations way ahead of time for special
events—You're not the only one
with parents.

89
Don't ask your parents for money—
Let them offer it to you.

90
Bring an iron.

91

When printing out your papers or assignments, use a good quality paper and keep your work neat—No matter how insignificant it may seem, it will have an impact on your grade as well as set you apart from the rest of the class.

92
Use a condom!—Nothing is worse than regret!

93
Bring coathangers—The dresser drawers are never big enough.

94
Don't join a cd club—You won't need
any more pressure.

95
Have a calculator.

96
Be in a good mood when it's parents weekend—School isn't exactly cheap!

97

Be nice to your housekeeping
crew–They keep your
room shiny clean.

98
If you have made holes in the walls, fill them in with toothpaste of the same color—Otherwise you will get fined for them.

99
Get an ATM bank card—They are good for last minute decisions.

100
Take courses that interest you—You will do much better in a course that you enjoy.

101
Bring packages of soup—They are cheap
and they taste great when you are sick.

102
Exercise—You can't study all of the time.

103
Decorate your room on holidays—It breaks the monotony.

104
Take a C.P.R. class—You may save a life!

105
Have a good thesaurus—It makes you sound like you know more than you actually do.

106
Make as few enemies as possible— Especially if you are going to a small school.

107
Be confident, yet not conceited—It will make others come to you.

108
Bring a stuffed animal—It will keep you company during lonely times.

109
Take a psychology class—Dealing with people is the key to success.

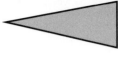

110
If you can't bring a vacuum cleaner, at least bring a dustbuster or a broom.

111
Bring an extra blanket—The heaters don't work that well and if they do, they come on at the wrong time.

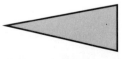

112
Be five minutes early when you are meeting with a professor—It shows that you care.

113
Keep an open mind—Anything is possible.

114
Don't skip breakfast—It keeps you awake during class.

115
Bring stick-up note pads—They are great for leaving messages.

116
First impressions last a lifetime!

117
Bring laundry detergent—And lots of it!

118
Look in the library first before you buy all of your books—It won't cost you anything to check them out.

119
If possible, try to get to school earlier than your roommate—First come, first serve!

120
Bring a water jug for fresh water and keep it in your refrigerator.

121
Don't buy all of your books at once—
Some professors never even use all
of them.

122
Learn how to take good notes—It is
one of the keys to good grades.

123
Be responsible for your actions.

124
Bring a raincoat.

125
If you are thinking about buying
a computer, purchase it through your
school. You'll save more money.

126
Get as much interview experience as possible—Your future may count on it.

127
Take time to waste time.

128

Bring pictures and posters to hang up in your room—You'll be there for a while, and chipped paint just doesn't do it.

129
Go to sporting events and support your school—It will help your school image.

130
Have a lot of highlighters.

131
Bring a lot of extra typing and printing ribbon—You always seem to run out at the worst times.

132
Bring cold medicines.

133
Don't get a tattoo—Unless you're sober.

134
Have a sturdy backpack.

135
Don't come to class more than ten minutes late.

136
Get and stay organized—Things will be easier, and they won't pile up as fast.

137
Bring Twister—It's a good study break and a great party game.

138
Call your future roommate—It is pointless to have two of everything.

139
Go to Colonial Inauguration–
Not only will you have the
option of choosing your future
roommate, but you'll find out
that you're all in the same boat.

140
Take a nice picture for your student
I.D.—Everyone will see it and you'll have
it for four years.

141
Bring a coffee mug.

142
Start building your resume—Be an active part in the community.

143
Don't give up your hobbies.

144
Don't be afraid to drop a class—A failing grade can really bring down your G.P.A.

145
Buy cheap beer.

146

If you are an athlete, get your sports physical the summer before you go to school—You'll never be able to get an appointment at school, and when you do, it's never convenient!

147
Have a good stapler and hide it in your drawer.

148
Bring microwave popcorn.

149

Know the campus before you pick the dorm that you are going to live in—It's nice to be close to the academic buildings when you're walking to them in the morning.

150
Avoid talking about or referring back to high-school—No one cares!

151
Have a message board for your door— It's nice to know who stopped by when you were gone.

152
Have a sewing kit and know how to use it—Your desk drawer will accumulate buttons awfully quick.

153
Write your grandparents—It doesn't have to be long and it will **PAY** off!

154
Have a good pocket knife with a bottle opener on it—It will come in very handy.

155
Unless you like taking cold showers, get to the bathroom first in the morning.

156
Bring some type of bathroom shoes or flip flops—Some very strange and slippery things grow on the shower floors.

157
Go on a road trip with a bunch of friends—It's nice to get away sometimes.

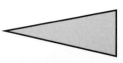

158
Bring vitamins—You won't get much sleep.

159
Pay your phone bill on time—Paying a ten dollar late fee for a nine dollar phone bill isn't very fun.

160

Start fresh—Be who you want to be. No one knows who you are and the only expectations are the ones that you put upon yourself!

161
Expect your midterm grades to be worse than they actually are—The professors just want you to work harder.

162
Buy a plant and put it in your room— It will make your room more homey and also add some life to it.

163
Go to class—You won't have to study as much for the tests.

164
Bring plastic cups.

165
Don't just study the night before
the exam—study in advance, it reduces
the stress.

166
Have a Walkman—Your roommate never
likes the same music as you do.

167
Build a loft—You will appreciate the extra space.

168
Take two pens to class—One of them will always explode at the wrong time.

169
Your happiness does not necessarily depend on the school itself, but on yourself!

170
Eat healthy—You'll look and feel better about yourself.

171
Get your best sleep two nights before a sporting event or final—It's more important than the night before.

172
Talk to your professors throughout the
semester—Don't be a face in the crowd.

173
Use your Career Development Center—
It is crucial to finding a job after college!

174
Bring two toothbrushes and lots of toothpaste.

175
Use all of the resources that you possibly can. That is what you are paying for.

176
Bring some type of air freshener—You're not the only person that has lived in that particular room.

177
Go on dates—Don't just go to parties.

178
Bring a bicycle—You won't have a lot of access to a car.

179
If you have roommate problems bring them out into the open or they will just get worse.

180
Meet as many people as possible.

181
Always have extra soap and a bottle of shampoo—Because everyone ends up using it.

182
Take an art class—It will give you a different perspective.

183
Have as many family members as possible bring you to school—It will help when you are moving all of your things into your room.

184
Don't put too much pressure on yourself—You'll never be able to relax.

185
Know your social security number—You will have to write it on everything.

186
Don't ride with someone who has been drinking!

187
Don't drive after you have been drinking!

188
Talk to your professor before each test or exam—Even if you know the material, they'll tell you exactly what is going to be on it.

189
Don't take your laundry home—
Be different.

190
Read your school newspaper—You won't be left in the dark and you'll always know what is happening on campus.

191
Do a rough draft even if you aren't asked to.

192
Join the local public library—Especially if it is bigger than your school library.

193
Don't sell back the books in your major—You'll need to refer back to them a lot.

194
If possible, help pay for your college
education—It will have more value
to you and you will work harder
because of it.

195
Don't put off getting measured for your
cap and gown—Trust me!

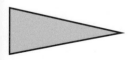
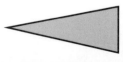

196
Bring a book to read for enjoyment.

197
Don't skip class during the first week of school—It will become a bad habit much too quickly.

198
Don't bring too much junk—The rooms aren't that big!

199
If you can, sell your books directly to students who are taking the same class the next semester—You will make more money and they will save more.

200
Don't give your parents <u>or sister</u>! any reason
to worry!

201
STUDY A LOT!

202
HAVE <u>FUN</u>!